Floyd Schofield Presents:

DIY FREE
Credit Repair

Trifecta Financials LLC

DO-IT YOUR SELF CREDIT REPAIR KIT

www.trifectafinancials.com

13010 Morris RD
Building 1
Alpharetta GA 30004
(678) 405-3001

Content

INTRODUCTION

We are a country in debt. Not only is our government in debt, but we, as Americans, are in debt ourselves, and the problem is just getting worse! Recent studies have shown that ninety percent of Americans have at least one credit card – and they are using that card – a lot! The average family carries a balance of between $7,000 and $10,000 on all their credit cards. Over $1,000 per family goes on interest every year. And that's just the average – some people owe much more!

Overall, Americans spend over 1 trillion dollars every year on their credit cards, and they owe more than 500 billion dollars of it. If debt continues at the current rate, then one family in a hundred will be forced into bankruptcy. Over 90% of Americans' disposable incomes are spent paying back debts. The truth is that you can get out of debt and repair your credit nearly to what it was before you had credit problems. It takes some time and a little work on your part, but it is possible.

Your credit score number is what determines if you can get credit, what your interest rate will be, and how much money potential lenders will give you. A good median score is 750, but the higher your score is, the more financially sound you are. While it's always a good idea to try and stay away from credit, not everyone has a hundred thousand dollars lying around to buy a home or twenty thousand to buy a car. Heck, for some people, scraping together five thousand dollars for a good used car is difficult; that is why we need credit.

Where the trouble comes in is when people begin to buy everyday items such as groceries and clothing on credit cards. Then those bills begin to get bigger and bigger until pretty soon, they're paying the minimum amount due which will take forever to pay off. Plus, a lot of people just continue charging things even when they have a large balance on their account.

Your credit score defines who you are to businesses and you want it to be as high as it can be. It doesn't matter how bad your credit is now. There are ways that you can raise your credit score no matter how low it is. Don't despair; just get started – right away!

Chapter 1
FIRST THINGS FIRST - YOUR CREDIT REPORT

The very first step you need to take when trying to raise your credit score is to find out what your score is and what it means. Legislation called "The Fact Act" was passed that allows all Americans to get one free copy of their credit report every year. This report lists all of your debts you've had and your payment history on those debts.

It will tell you where you owe money, how much you owe, and how you pay (on time, 30 days late, etc.). All of that information is compiled together and then analyzed. After the analysis, a number is assigned to you as to what your credit fitness level is. Potential creditors then look at your credit score and decide if you are going to be able to pay back the amount of money you are requesting to borrow.

That's the short version. Actually, there is much, much more involved in determining your credit score. However, what should be important to you knows how to read your credit report and how to raise that score so that you are able to get the things you need. Remember that – the things you NEED, not the things you WANT!

Let's start with how to get your credit report in the first place. There are three major credit reporting agencies that will offer you the one free credit report you get each year. They are Experian, TransUnion, and Equifax. You can contact each of them directly in the following ways:

- **Equifax** – Online, you can find them at www.equifax.com. You can also order your free credit report by mail. However, they only offer this option for free to residents in the states of Colorado, Georgia, Maine, Maryland, Massachusetts, New Jersey, and Vermont. All other states are required to pay a $10 fee.

  If you do want to do this by mail, send your request to Equifax Information Services LLC. Disclosure Department, P.O. Box 740241 Atlanta, GA 30374. You can also call them at 1-800-685-1111.

- **TransUnion** – Their web address is www.transunion.com. As with Equifax, you can also make your request via mail by getting a copy of their mail request form online and sending it to the address provided. You can also call them at 1-877-322-8228.

- **Experian** – www.experian.com is where you can make a request for a credit report from this credit reporting agency. As with TransUnion, you will need to download a form from their website if you wish to request your credit report by mail. By phone you can call 888 397 3742.

There is also a myriad of websites who will also allow you to download your free credit report, but they ultimately will just be forwarding you to one of the above websites anyway. However, they are worth checking out for the information that you can find on them. Here are a few:

- www.annualcreditreport.com
- www.freecreditreport.com
- www.creditreport.com
- www.freecreditreportinstantly.com

The main thing is that you will want to get your free credit report in order to find out where you stand and how far you have to go to repair your credit. Most of the time when you download your credit report, you will be able to view and save it instantly. Save it to your computer "My Documents" file if you can. That way you will be able to print it out and refer to it as much as you need. Also, some of these sites offer low-cost memberships that will alert you if a new item comes onto your credit report. Their services will offer many different things, but purchasing a membership is strictly voluntary and probably not necessary if you want the straight truth.

Once you get a copy of your credit report, it's important to know how to read it. There are going to be an awful lot of numbers, abbreviations and terms you've never seen before. Trade lines, charge-offs, account review, inquiries – how do you read this thing? Even though you get one free credit report each year, experts suggest that if you are serious about improving your credit score, you need to examine a report from each of the three major credit reporting agencies. This will, however cost you a small fee from the other two, so keep that in mind.

Why do they suggest you have all three? Creditors can pick and choose which credit reporting agency they want to report to. Some will report to all three, but many won't. You may find that what is included on one report isn't on another. The reports will have different information because it's a voluntary system, and creditors subscribe to whichever agency they want – if any at all.

A credit report is basically divided into four sections: identifying information, credit history, public records and inquiries. Identifying information is just that -- information to identify you. Look at it closely to make sure it's accurate. It's not unusual for there to be two or three spellings of your name or more than one Social Security number. That's usually because someone reported the information that way. Dispute that inaccurate information and remove it from your credit report.

Other information in this section might include your current and previous addresses, your date of birth, telephone numbers, driver's license numbers, your employer and your spouse's name. The data in this section is often used to verify your identity or to confirm that the information you provided for an application is accurate. Small variations in this data between the three bureaus are normal as each agency may have their own recording procedures.

The personal information section of your credit report may also include a "consumer statement." This is a statement that you asked the credit reporting agencies to add to your report. Commonly, this statement is used to explain a record on your report. For example, "The Smith Bank account from 2004 was a shared account with my ex-husband." This statement does not impact your credit score but may help you clarify a situation to a potential creditor or lender and improve your chances to obtain credit. The next section is your credit history. Sometimes, the individual accounts are called trade lines. Each account will include the name of the creditor and the account number, which may be scrambled for security purposes.

You may have more than one account from a creditor. Many creditors have more than one kind of account, or if you move, they transfer your account to a new location and assign a new number. The entry will also include:

- When you opened the account

- The kind of credit (installment, such as a mortgage or car loan, or revolving, such as a department store credit card)
- Whether the account is in your name alone or with another person
- Total amount of the loan, high credit limit or highest balance on the card
- How much you still owe
- Fixed monthly payments or minimum monthly amount
- Status of the account (open, inactive, closed, paid, etc.)
- How well you've paid the account

On Experian's report, your payment history is written in plain English -- never pays late, typically pays 30 days late, etc. Other comments might include internal collection and charged off or default. Charged off means the creditor has given up, thrown in the towel. Basically, the company has made efforts to collect the debt, realized that it's not going to be paid, and subsequently wrote it off.

Other reports use payment codes ranging from 1 to 9; an R1 or I1 on a report is an indication of a good payment history on a revolving or installment account. Often, the code key will be listed on the report so you can better understand what the codes mean, but they may not.

Credit accounts are divided into five categories: real estate, installment, revolving, collection and other. Here is a better description of each category:

Real Estate: first and second mortgage loans on your home.
Installment: Accounts comprised of fixed terms with regular payments, such as a car loan.
Revolving: Accounts with opened terms with varying payments, such as a credit card account.
Collection: Accounts seriously past due that have been assigned to an attorney or collection agency.
Other: Accounts where the exact category is unknown. This could include 30-day accounts, such as an American Express card.

Your credit report lists a summary of the details and terms for each account. This summary includes information about the account number, condition, balance, type and pay status for each account. The summary for collection records is slightly different.

The following information is for real estate, installment, revolving and other type records:

- **Creditor**: The official account name. This name may be different than you expect if your account is managed by a larger financial corporation.
- **Account Number**: This is an identifying number for your account. Typically, this would be a credit card number for a credit card account or a loan identification number for a mortgage. A portion of the number is hidden for security reasons. A partial account number is all that is needed to file a dispute about the record.
- **Condition**: This is the account's status as open or closed, according to the most recent update from your creditor.
- **Balance**: The amount you presently owe on the account based on the last reported activity. Very recent activities may not yet have appeared in the bureaus' computer system so this balance may be a few days out-of-date.
- **Type**: The account's specific type. Some common types are real estate, automobile, educational and credit card accounts.
- **Pay Status**: The account's payment status, according to the most recent update from your creditor.

For each account, the report also displays an illustrated payment history over the last 24 months. There will be a key at the top of this section describes each payment history symbol and what it indicates for your account. Green boxes marked "OK" show that your payment was made on time.

Most credit reports also give you more in-depth information about specific accounts. This is also an important part of the credit report you'll want to review for accuracy. The following information may be reported for your account in this section:

- **Past Due**: The amount of payment overdue as of the most recent reported activity. Very recent payments may take a few days to appear on your credit report.
- **High Balance**: The most you have ever owed on this account. In the case of a credit card, this is the highest balance you've ever charged. For a mortgage, it is the initial amount of the mortgage.
- **Terms**: This is the number of payments you have scheduled with a creditor. Most commonly this applies to loan accounts.

For example, an auto loan may have a repayment plan scheduled over 36 months and a home loan may have a repayment plan scheduled over 360 months.

- **Limits**: For a credit card or other revolving account, this is the maximum amount you are approved to borrow.
- **Payment**: This is the minimum amount you are required to pay each month toward the account.
- **Opened**: The date the account was opened.
- **Reported**: The last date when any activity for this account was shown. Activities include payments, credit card billings and changes in your terms. Very recent activity may not yet show on your account, since it takes time for it to appear in the credit reporting agency's system.
- **Responsibility**: This indicates your responsibility for the account for example individual, joint, or co-signer.
- **Late Payments**: A summary of your 30, 60, and 90-day late payments over the past 7 years. Please note that the figures in the "seven year" history include any late payments shown in the two-year history.
- **Remarks**: Notes about the status or condition of your account.
  Collection accounts are accounts that are seriously past due and have been transferred to an attorney, collection agency, or creditor's internal collection agency. As your debt is transferred between different agencies, you may see several records on your report for the same debt.

Only one record should be marked as open at a time. All the collection records and the original debt record will expire from your credit report at the same time. Collection records use a unique summary format on your credit report:

- **Creditor Name**: The official name of the company that is currently attempting to collect the debt.
- **Account Number**: An identifying number for your account with the collection agency. This is not the same as the account number on your original debt.
- **Original Creditor**: The name of the original creditor where you accumulated your debt. This could be an account that is listed on your credit report (such as a credit card) or an account that is not listed on your report (such as a library, video rental or cell phone company). If this creditor was a medical office, the name may be masked for your privacy.

- **Responsibility**: This indicates your responsibility for the account, for example individual, joint, or co-signer.
- **Condition**: The current status of your collection record, for example open, closed or paid.
- **Original Balance**: The amount of debt owed on the original account before it was transferred.
- **Date Opened**: The date the account was transferred to the collection agency.
- **Date Reported**: The date of the collection agency's last update to this account record.
- **Remarks**: Notes about the account as reported to each credit reporting agency. This section may note that the collector has been unable to locate you or that you have not yet paid the debt.

The next section is the part you want to be absolutely blank. The public records section is never a good story. If you have a public record on there, you've had a problem that has required litigation. It doesn't list arrests and criminal activities; just financial-related data, such as bankruptcies, judgments and tax liens. Those are the monsters that will trash your credit faster than anything else.

Here are definitions of the eight types of public records you could see listed on your credit report:

- **Bankruptcy**: A legal filing that relieves a person of responsibility for all or some of their debts because they are unable to pay.
- **Tax Lien**: A claim filed by a local, state or federal tax agency against a person who owes back taxes.
- **Legal Item**: A general filing. This is most commonly a judgment against you in civil action.
- **Marital Item**: A legal filing related to a marital or divorce issue.
- **Financial Counseling**: A public record indicating that a person has participated in financial counseling.
- **Financial Statement**: A type of lien filed by a creditor against a person's property. This can be filed when a loan is secured against personal property.
- **Foreclosure**: A record indicating that a mortgaged property has been taken over by the creditor because the borrower has defaulted on the loan.

- **Garnishment**: A record indicating a court order to withhold some or all of a person's wages to repay a debt owed to a creditor.

The summary information listed for each of these types of public records can vary. Here are some definitions of common record categories:

- **Type**: The type of record, for example a tax lien, bankruptcy, garnishment, or judgment.
- **Status**: Current status of the record, for example released, filed or dismissed.
- **Date Filed/Reported**: Date when the record was initially filed or created.
- **How Filed**: The role that you played in the public record. Usually the record is filed either individually or jointly.
- **Reference Number:** Identifying number for the record.

- **Released/Closing Date:** Date when the record was closed, released or judgment was awarded.

- **Court:** The court or legal agency that has jurisdiction over the record.

- **Plaintiff:** The plaintiff in the case of a legal judgment.

- **Amount:** Dollar amount of the lien or judgment.

- **Remarks:** Notes regarding the public record as reported to the credit bureaus. If the public record is a bankruptcy, three other fields will be visible.

- **Liability:** The amount the court found you to be legally responsible to repay.

- **Exempt Amount:** The dollar amount claimed against you that the court has decided you are not legally responsible for.

- **Asset Amount:** The dollar amount of total personal assets used in the court's decision. The Asset Amount can include items of value that can be used to pay debts.

The final section is the inquiries. That's a list of everyone who asked to see your credit report. That means if you try to apply for a credit card, it's listed as an inquiry. Have you been shopping for a car? Every time a dealership runs a credit report, it shows. If you call the credit bureau and ask for a copy, it will be on there.

It's a very detailed entry record. Inquiries are divided into two sections. "Hard" inquiries are ones you initiate by filling out a credit application or taking your child to the orthodontist. "Soft" inquiries are from companies that want to send out promotional information to a pre-qualified group or current creditors who are monitoring your account.

You may have heard that a large number of inquiries can have a negative impact on your credit score, but you're probably OK. The vast majority of inquiries are ignored by the fICO scoring models. For instance, the model has a buffer period that ignores inquiries within 30 days of getting a mortgage or a car loan.
It also counts two or more "hard" inquiries in the same 14-day period as just one inquiry. You could have 30 in two weeks and it only counts as one.

However, on the other hand, having a lot of credit inquiries on your account could also show potential creditors that you are trying to live your life on credit which means you might not have the means to pay back the debt. This is especially true if you've been applying for a lot of credit cards. And there are always many opportunities to apply for a credit card. They usually read "You've Been Approved!" as an enticement for filling out the application. This is not always true with pre-approval offers, so proceed carefully.

Another time that you will be asked to apply for credit occurs in public places and the companies are offering products for free in exchange for a credit application. Keep an eye out for your favorite department stores. They have store credit cards and may offer you a percentage off your purchase in exchange for a credit application. In general, this is not a bad idea – which we will talk about a little later in rebuilding your credit – because store credit cards are great when rebuilding your credit.

The bottom line is that if you don't need another credit card, don't apply for one. It's always good to have one on hand for emergencies. But having five or six can just be a temptation to spend beyond your means.

There may also be a section on your credit report that lists creditor information. The creditor contact section lists the name and contact information for each creditor that appears on your credit report. This can also include the contact information for creditors that have made inquiries.

Each creditor's address is listed to the right of the creditor's name. When available, a phone number is listed for the creditor. Creditors without listed numbers should be contacted by mail.

So that's the first step – getting your credit report and going over it with a fine-tooth comb. But where's that magic number – your credit score? let's begin with a short section on the credit score itself and where it comes from.

Chapter 2

Fico and You

Back in the 1960's, a company called fair Isaac, devised a unique system to determine the credit worthiness of people who apply for loans. Through a complicated mathematical computation, they were able to study a person's credit history and assign them a number that would represent how likely it was that they would be able to repay a loan they were applying for.

Fair Isaac sparked a revolution by pioneering credit risk scoring for the financial services industry. This new approach to lending enabled financial institutions to improve their business performance and expand consumers' access to credit. Today fair Isaac's fICO score is widely recognized as the industry standard for lenders.

The fICO score condenses a borrower's credit history into a single number based on past credit history. Fair, Isaac & Co. and the credit bureaus do not reveal how these scores are computed. The federal trade commission has ruled this to be acceptable. Credit scores are calculated by using scoring models and mathematical tables that assign points for different pieces of information which best predict future credit performance. Developing these models involves studying how thousands, even millions, of people have used credit.

Score-model developers find predictive factors in the data that have proven to indicate future credit performance. Models can be developed from different sources of data. Credit-bureau models are developed from information in consumer credit-bureau reports.

Credit scores analyze a borrower's credit history considering numerous factors such as:

- Late payments
- The amount of time credit has been established
- The amount of credit used versus the amount of credit available
- Length of time at present residence

- Negative credit information such as bankruptcies, charge-offs, collections, etc.

There are really three fICO scores computed by data provided by each of the three bureaus—Experian, Trans Union and Equifax. Some lenders use one of these three scores, while other lenders may just use the middle score.

Fair Isaac has become so important in the financial industry that their word on your credit has become basically the final word. Why would banks and creditors place so much credibility into one company? The answer is simply because of their proven track record.

The fico score has proven to be not only an accurate and amazingly consistent way of showing a person's credit reliability, but it has also saved companies millions of dollars in credit write-offs due to bad lending decisions. A study of loans that were granted and/or denied simply due to the fico scores shows that fair Isaac has been right over 80 percent of the time.

Of course, that required some chance taking on the part of many creditors, but they were willing to take the risk. After all, this was a ground-breaking thing determining credit worthiness through a simple three-digit number. Many companies jumped "on the bandwagon" just to show that fair Isaac had the right idea.

Fast forward to the twenty-first century and you will find that fico has become the definitive when it comes to financial and credit matters. They have proven their reliability and their worthiness just through trial and error.

Unfortunately, the problem is that finding your fico score isn't as easy as you think. The truth is that it's not even shown on your credit report like you would think. In fact, for years and years, your credit score was a securely kept secret number that was elusive to the average person.

So how can you find out your credit score? When I first started, I spent about thirty minutes trying to figure out how to find my own credit score. It wasn't as easy as I thought it would be. But thanks to my tireless research, I can help you find your score.

Chapter 3
NEXT THINGS NEXT - FINDING YOUR SCORE

You would think that finding out what your credit score is would be easy. In a way it is, but only because I've done my research and you won't have to spend time surfing websites looking for the ever-elusive credit number. It would seem logical to have your credit score appear right on your credit report, but that's just not the way it is.

At one time, your credit score was a big secret known only to financial companies and banks. With the FACT Act, legislators decided that it was important for individuals to know not only what their personal credit scores are but how they are calculated and how to improve them.

The main company who calculates your credit score is the field, Isaac company commonly known as FICO. They invented the concept of the FICO scores, so they are the ones who are known as experts in the industry. Before we go into finding your score, let's look at a few facts about the FICO score.

- FICO scores are your credit rating
- They range from 300-850
- Most lenders base approval on them
- Higher scores mean lower interest rates
- FICO scores are calculated based on your rating in five general categories:
  o Payment history - 35%
  o Amounts owed - 30%
  o length of credit history - 15%
  o New credit - 10%
  o Types of credit used - 10%
- Field, Isaac Company is the inventor of the FICO score
- They have the only website offering all 3 of your FICO scores
- The median FICO score in the U.S. is 723

Essentially, your credit score is simply a snapshot of your credit use -- it's the Cliffs Notes version of seven years of your borrowing history. In many lending situations, the lender bases its decision almost solely on your credit score. Consider your credit score the overall GPA of your borrowing history.

Now, here's the bad news. If you want to know your actual credit score, you will usually have to purchase it. This can be done in a few ways.

You can get it from one of the three major credit reporting companies: Equifax, Experian, and TransUnion. The fee isn't a huge one – usually around $15 or $20. However, if you're serious about growing your credit score, it's well worth the money to be financially responsible in the end.

You can also go to www.myfico.com and get your FICO score directly from them. They will offer you a free 30-day trial membership which will get your credit score right now and then, if you wish to continue the membership, it will update the score as it rises (or, heaven forbid lowers).

If you are applying for a mortgage, here's a little good news for you. You can find out your credit score for free! The mortgage company will base their decision and interest rate on what your credit score number is, so just ask and they'll tell you!

FICO scores range between 300 and 850. Here's what those scores mean:

- Over 750 – you have excellent credit and will be able obtain credit easily
- 720 or more – you still have very good credit and will be able to obtain credit easily
- 660 to 720 – this is an acceptable credit. You can still get loans, but you may pay a higher interest rate
- 620 to 660 – creditors are going to be uncertain about lending you money
- Less than 620 – you have poor credit history and will probably not be able to obtain credit on your own.

Knowing the above information makes it obvious that if you need or want to get credit for something, the higher your score is, the better your chances are to not only get credit but get it at a handsome interest rate. If you are in the 660 to 620 range, you may still get a loan, but the interest rate is likely to be higher. That's why it's important to keep your credit good or establish good credit from the beginning.

Chapter 4
ESTABLISHING GOOD CREDIT

This is one of the most important steps, especially while you are young. The chances of you needing credit in the future are very real. Someday you might want to buy a house, or you may want to buy a new car. Chances are pretty good that you won't have the cash outright to buy these "high ticket" items, which mean you will need credit. Plus, it's always good to have a little credit since many utility companies will look at your credit to turn on your power bill, for example, without a deposit of some type. When you're starting fresh with no credit history at all, here are a few ways to get a good start on establishing good credit:

Pay your bills on time, especially mortgage or rent payments - **Apart from extreme circumstances like bankruptcy or tax liens, nothing has as big of an impact on your credit history as late payments.**

Establish credit early - **Having clean, active charge accounts established many years ago will boost your score. If you are averse to credit, on principle, consider setting up automatic monthly payments for, say, utilities and phone on a credit card account and locking the card away where it's not a temptation.**

Don't max out available credit on credit card accounts - **Lenders won't be impressed. Instead, they are much more likely to assume that you have trouble managing your finances. Beyond one or two credit cards, it starts to get complicated.**

Don't apply for too much credit in a short amount of time - **Multiple requests for your credit history (not including requests by you to check your file) will reduce your score. If you are hunting around for good loan rates, assume that every time you give your Social Security number to a lender or credit card company, they will order a credit history.**

Be neat and consistent when filling out credit applications - **This will ensure that all your good deeds get recorded in a single file, as opposed to multiple files or, worse, someone else's file. Watch out for inconsistencies in use of "Jr." and "Sr."**

Check your credit history for errors - especially if you will soon be requesting a time-dependent loan, like a mortgage.

One great way to start establishing credit is to apply for a store credit card (Sears, JC Penney, Macys etc.). Once you get the card, make a few small purchases and pay them off completely. Do this a few times over the course of a year and you'll find yourself with some established credit with an excellent payment history. DO NOT go overboard and buy more than what you can pay for.

You can also apply for a secured credit card. These cards ask that you place a certain amount of money in your account for which you will receive a charge card. Then you can make purchases up to the amount of money that is in your account. Credit reporting agencies treat these cards just like regular credit cards and look to them as a responsible way for you to establish a good credit history.

You will have to have a checking account to establish credit. This lends to your credibility with lenders and shows that you are able to manage your money effectively.

When applying for a credit card of any type, be sure to ask if they report to any of the credit reporting agencies. As we've said before, they are not required to do so, and if they don't, having one of these cards or loans won't do you a lick of good even if you do make your payments on time.

You can also establish credit by making a purchase or applying for a loan with a co-signer. A co-signer is a person with good credit history who is basically telling the lending company that they will be responsible for making sure you make your payments on time. Often a co-signer is a relative such as a parent. This can be a risky proposition for them, so know that they are putting their own credit history on the line just to help you out, so don't let them down.

When applying for a loan, such as a car loan, it can also be helpful if you have a large down payment to make thus lessening the amount of money you have to borrow. This shows the lending company that you have the ability to save and they are more likely to take a chance on you based on this factor alone.

Here is a quick review on how to establish a good credit history:

- Apply for a store or gas credit card and make a few charges
- Ask a loved one to co-sign on a loan

- Find a respected secured credit card company
- Open a checking account
- Don't apply for too many credit cards in too short of a time
- Check your credit report for any errors
- Go slowly
- Don't overspend
- Make sure your lender reports to at least one of the credit reporting agencies
- MAKE YOUR PAYMENTS ON TIME!!!!!!!

Of course, the last one is the most important in establishing credit. If you don't make your payments on time, it wouldn't make a difference what you are trying to do. This is what makes your credit history worthwhile – making on time payments and showing you are responsible with your credit to your creditors.

So, what if you've already had credit, but you've made some mistakes over the years finding yourself with bad credit? Is all hope lost? The good news is – NO!

Chapter 5
REPAIRING YOUR CREDIT SCORE

Don't despair if you find yourself with a less than desirable credit score and credit history. You are human and can make mistakes, it is natural. The key to this is recognizing that your spending habits are out of control; your credit has been damaged; and then vow to never get yourself back in the same situation after you have gotten your credit repaired.

The first step is to get your credit report. You get one free and then you will probably have to pay around $10 a piece for the other two. It's important to get reports from all three agencies so that you have a full picture of your credit history. Some companies only report to one agency; some report to all three. But if you are committed to repairing your credit, you need all three so that you don't miss anything.
Next, go over those credit reports carefully. See the section above on how to read your credit reports. Check to see that there are no errors such as a bill you've paid but that is still being shown as owed.

People at credit bureaus are human too and make mistakes just like you! If you don't call attention to these mistakes, no one else will. We will cover correcting those mistakes a little bit later. The next part involves pulling out those accounts that are delinquent and making a re-payment plan. Unless you are declaring bankruptcy, you will still need to pay your debts and doing so can go a long way towards improving your credit history. Creditors will see that you are doing the best you can to get back on your feet and this improves your credibility.

If all the bills are too overwhelming for you to consider paying back at once, just concentrate on one at a time. Break them into pieces, contact the company and let them know you are trying to come up with a repayment plan and if there's anything they can do to help you out.

These companies really just want their money in the long run, so they are going to be willing to help you. Once that company is paid off, move on to the next one until everyone is paid off.

After that happens, it's not like your credit is immediately pristine. Late payments and charged-off accounts remain on your report for seven years. Most creditors, however, look for a pattern of payment rather than focusing on one-time or rare occurrences. That's why consistent on-time bill payments will improve those blemishes.

As soon as you have paid off your creditors, then you can start all over again. Nothing can compare to consistent, on-time bill payments and responsible credit practices when it comes to repairing your credit. Experts say the average time required to rebuild one's credit to the point at which you can be accepted for a major credit card or small loan is approximately two years.

Here are some other things to consider when trying to repair your credit:

- Pay down your credit cards - Paying off your installment loans (mortgage, auto, student, etc.) can help your score, but typically not as dramatically as paying down -- or paying off -- revolving accounts like credit cards. The credit-scoring formulas like to see a nice, big gap between the amount of credit you're using and your available credit limits. Getting your balances below 30% of the credit limit on each card can really help.

  While most debt gurus recommend paying off the highest-rate card first, a better strategy here is to pay down the cards that are closest to their limits.

- Use your cards lightly - Racking up big balances can hurt your score, regardless of whether you pay your bill in full each month. What's typically reported to the credit bureaus, and thus calculated into your score, is the balance reported on your last statement. That doesn't mean paying off your balances each month isn't financially smart -- it is -- just that the credit score doesn't care.

  You typically can increase your score by limiting your charges to 30% or less of a card's limit. If you're having trouble keeping track, consider using a check register to track your spending, logging into your account frequently at the issuer's Web site, or using personal finance software like Microsoft Money or Quicken, which can download your transactions and balances automatically.

- Check your limits - Your score might be artificially depressed if your lender is showing a lower limit than you've actually got. Most credit-card issuers will quickly update this information if you ask.

  If your issuer makes it a policy not to report consumers' limits, however -- as is the usual case with American Express cards and those issued by Capital One -- the bureaus typically use your highest balance as a proxy for your credit limit.

  You may see the problem here: If you consistently charge the same amount each month -- say $2,000 to $2,500 -- it may look to the credit-scoring formula like you're regularly maxing out that card.

  You could go on a wild spending spree to raise the limit, but a more sober solution would simply be to pay your balance down or off before your statement period closes.

  Check your last statement to see which day of the month that typically is, then go to the issuer's Web site about a week in advance of closing and pay off what you owe. It won't raise your reported limit, but it will widen the gap between that limit and your closing balance, which should boost your score.

- **Dust off an old card.** The older your credit history, the better. But if you stop using your oldest cards, the issuers may stop updating those accounts at the credit bureaus. The accounts will still appear, but they won't be given as much weight in the credit-scoring formula as your active accounts. That's why many financial companies recommend to their clients that they use their oldest cards every few months to charge a small amount, paying it off in full when the statement arrives.

- **Get some goodwill.** If you've been a good customer, a lender might agree to simply erase that one late payment from your credit history. You usually have to make the request in writing, and your chances for a "goodwill adjustment" improve the better your record with the company (and the better your credit in general). But it can't hurt to ask.

  A longer-term solution for more-troubled accounts is to ask that they be "re-aged." If the account is still open, the lender might erase previous delinquencies if you make a series of 12 or so on-time payments.

When trying to improve your credit score or credit history, avoid any of the following:

- **Asking a creditor to lower your credit limits** - This will reduce that all-important gap between your balances and your available credit, which could hurt your score. If a lender asks you to close an account or get a limit lowered as a condition for getting a loan, you might have to do it -- but don't do so without being asked.

- **Making a late payment** - The irony here is that a late or missed payment will hurt a good score more than a bad one, dropping a 700-plus score by 100 points or more. If you've already got a string of negative items on your credit report, one more won't have a big impact, but it's still something you want to avoid if you're trying to improve your score.

- **Consolidating your accounts** - Applying for a new account can ding your score. So, too, can transferring balances from a high-limit card to a lower-limit one, or concentrating all or most of your credit-card balances onto a single card. In general, it's better to have smaller balances on a few cards than a big balance on one.

- **Applying for new credit if you've already got plenty** - On the other hand, applying for and getting an installment loan can help your score if you don't have any installment accounts, or you're trying to recover from a credit disaster like bankruptcy.

By the way, all these suggestions work best if you have poor or mediocre scores to begin with. Once you've hit the 700 mark, any tweaking you do will tend to have less of a positive impact.

And if your scores are in the "excellent" category, 760 or above, you'll probably be able to eke out only a few extra points despite your best efforts.

There's really no point, anyway, since you're already qualified for the best rates and terms. Here's one area where it's really OK to rest on your laurels and worry about something else.

Chapter 6
Bankruptcy

Filing for bankruptcy has a very negative connotation in society, but it's a way for people who have found themselves in serious financial trouble to ease the burden of what they've done and allow them to start over. Businesses don't like it, but for consumers, it can be a life saver.

This writer knows of one young girl – just 21 years old – who was over $20,000 in debt plus she had her car repossessed for non-payment. At this young age, she was in serious financial trouble with no way out.

She was (still is) going to school trying to earn a degree so she can get a good job, but since her first credit card was issued to her at age 17, her credit woes began, and they didn't end until she was able to file for bankruptcy.

Her debts were discharged, and she was able to start all over again. She purchased a used vehicle for cash, got a part-time job while she went to school, and worked very hard to build her credit up slowly.

Now she is 30. She has a well-paying job as a nurse at a local hospital and just celebrated buying her first home. She once told me, "I knew I was in over my head and I became very depressed because of it. The bankruptcy was the best thing I could have ever done for myself even though at the time, it was the hardest."

Let's start by exploring the different types of bankruptcies. There are three different filings you can make: Chapter 7, Chapter 11, and Chapter 13.

Chapter 7 Bankruptcy

Chapter 7 bankruptcy sometimes call a straight bankruptcy is a liquidation proceeding. The debtor turns over all non-exempt property to the bankruptcy trustee who then converts it to cash for distribution to the creditors.

The debtor receives a discharge of all dischargeable debts usually within four months. In the vast majority of cases the debtor has no assets that he would lose so Chapter 7 will give that person a relatively quick "fresh start".

One of the main purposes of Bankruptcy law is to give a person, who is hopelessly burdened with debt, a fresh start by wiping out his or her debts.

New legislation has been passed regarding Chapter 7 bankruptcies. Laws can vary from state to state, so you will want to check with someone who knows or do extensive research as to what is allowed to be discharged with a Chapter 7 and what is not.

Essentially what the new laws ask of people who are filing a Chapter 7 bankruptcy is two-fold. First, they must take an approved credit counseling course within six months before filing. They must also complete an approved financial management course before any debts can be discharged.

Even though those two new stipulations are in place, it is still relatively easy to file for a Chapter 7 bankruptcy. There are, of course, governmental "hoops" you will have to jump through which is why it is often a good idea to secure the services of a bankruptcy lawyer. However, it is possible for you to do this yourself as long as you do your research and "cross your T's and dot your I's"!

What are the most common reasons given for filing a Chapter 7 bankruptcy? Well, of course, it's the accumulation of excessive debt! But seriously, here are the most common reasons why people get into such debt:

- Medical bills
- Unemployment
- Divorce
- Overextended credit
- large, unexpected expense

A Harvard Study reported that half of US bankruptcies were caused by medical bills. The study was published online in February of 2005 by Health Affairs. The Harvard study concluded that illness and medical bills caused half (50.4 percent) of the 1,458,000 personal bankruptcies in 2001. The study estimates that medical bankruptcies affect about 2 million Americans annually — counting debtors and their dependents, including about 700,000 children.

If you find that you have to file for a Chapter 7 bankruptcy, you may be worried about whether or not you'll get to keep some of the things that are important to you and essential to life. These things include a car and your home, among other things.

Unsecured debts, such as credit card debt, personal loans, money judgments and certain taxes are wiped out in a Chapter 7. However, certain debts are not dischargeable under Chapter 7 bankruptcy; these debts include, but are not limited to, most student loans, certain taxes, alimony and child or other court ordered support payments.

If a debt is secured by property, such as a home mortgage or an automobile loan, then you get to decide how to handle that debt. For example, in the case of a vehicle, you could:

- Keep the automobile and the debt as long as you are current and continue keeps your payments current.

- "Redeem" the automobile which means pay it off at its current "fair market value"

- Return the vehicle, include any balance due in your bankruptcy and pay nothing further on the vehicle; the choice is yours.

In 99% of the Chapter 7 cases, the person filing bankruptcy keeps all of their property. Bankruptcy law is not meant to punish you and allows you to keep your property under what are called "exemptions" or things you get to keep. You keep your car, your house, your jewelry, the boat, your clothing, everything!

Of course, if you still owe a debt on anything like your car and your house, you should refer to the above scenario. If you want to discharge your car loan, you'll have to either pay up or give up the car.

Chapter 13 Bankruptcy

Another option for bankruptcy for individuals is the Chapter 13. This is more commonly known as a reorganization bankruptcy. Chapter 13 bankruptcy is filed by individuals who want to pay off their debts over a period of three to five years.

This type of bankruptcy appeals to individuals who have non-exempt property that they want to keep. It is also only an option for individuals who have predictable income and whose income is sufficient to pay their reasonable expenses with some amount left over to pay off their debts.

There are many reasons why people choose Chapter 13 bankruptcy instead of Chapter 7 bankruptcy. Generally, you are probably a good candidate for Chapter 13 bankruptcy if you are in any of the following situations:

1. You have a sincere desire to repay your debts, but you need the protection of the bankruptcy court to do so. You may think filing Chapter 13 bankruptcy is simply the "Right Thing to Do" rather than file Chapter 7.
2. You are behind on your mortgage or car loan and want to make up the missed payments over time and reinstate the original agreement. You cannot do this in Chapter 7 bankruptcy. You can make up missed payments only in Chapter 13 bankruptcy.
3. You need help repaying your debts now but need to leave open the option of filing for Chapter 7 bankruptcy in the future. This would be the case if for some reason you can't stop incurring new debt.
4. You are a family farmer who wants to pay off your debts, but you do not qualify for a Chapter 12 family farming bankruptcy because you have a large debt unrelated to farming.
5. You have valuable nonexempt property. When you file for Chapter 7 bankruptcy, you get to keep certain property, called exempt. If you have a lot of nonexempt property (which you'd have to give up if you file a Chapter 7 bankruptcy), Chapter 13 bankruptcy may be the better option.
6. You received a Chapter 7 discharge within the previous eight years. You cannot file for Chapter 7 again until the eight years are up.

A Chapter 13 can be filed if:

- The debtor received a discharge under Chapter 7, 11 or 12 more than four years ago
- The debtor received a discharge under Chapter 13 more than two years ago.
- You have a co-debtor on a personal debt. If you file for Chapter 7 bankruptcy, your creditor will go after the co-debtor for payment. If you file for Chapter 13 bankruptcy, the creditor will leave your co-debtor alone, as long as you keep up with your bankruptcy plan payments.
- You have a tax debt. If a large part of your debt consists of federal taxes, what happens to your tax debts may determine which type of bankruptcy is best for you.

As of October 17, 2005, new bankruptcy laws took effect for all three types of bankruptcy. When it comes to Chapter 13, you cannot file this way unless the following conditions are met:

- The debtor received a discharge under Chapter 7, 11 or 12 more than four years ago.
- The debtor received a discharge under Chapter 13 more than two years ago.
- When a motor vehicle was purchased within 910 days (2 1/2 years) of the filing and a secured creditor has a lien on it, the creditor retains the lien until payment of the entire debt has been made.
- The following debt is NOT discharged:

    1. Debt for trust fund taxes
    2. Taxes for which returns were never filed or filed late (within two years of the petition date)
    3. Taxes for which the debtor made a fraudulent return or evaded taxes;
    4. Domestic support payments
    5. Student loans
    6. Drunk driving injuries
    7. Criminal restitution
    8. Civil restitutions or damages awarded for willful or malicious personal actions causing personal injury or death.

- All tax returns for the four years prior to filing Chapter 13 must be filed.
- Debtors must provide to the trustee, at least seven days prior to the 341 meeting, a copy of a tax return or transcript of a tax return, for the period for which the return was most recently due.

Chapter 11 Bankruptcy

A Chapter 11 bankruptcy is filed by businesses and is quite similar to a Chapter 13. A Chapter 11 is available for individuals, but it is generally used by businesses to reorganize their debts and dealings so that they can be more financially solid.

When a troubled business is unable to service its debt or pay its creditors, they can file with a federal bankruptcy court for protection under either a Chapter 7 or a Chapter 11 bankruptcy.

In a Chapter 7 bankruptcy, the business must cease operation and a trustee will sell all its assets and distribute the proceeds to the business's creditors ratably in accordance with statutory priorities.

A Chapter 11 filing, on the other hand, is usually filed in an attempt to stay in business while a bankruptcy court supervises the reorganization of the company's contractual and debt obligations. The court can grant complete or partial relief from most of the company's debts along with its contracts so that the company can make a fresh start.

Often, if the company's debts exceed its assets, then at the completion of the bankruptcy, the company's owners or stockholders all end up with nothing. All their rights and interests are terminated, and the company's creditors end up with ownership of the newly reorganized company in the hopes that it will eventually succeed financially as compensation for their losses.

So, in general, an individual bankruptcy will be under a Chapter 7 or Chapter 11. It's a big decision for you to make, but sometimes, it's the only way you can "get out from under" and begin anew.

Before you resort to filing for a Chapter 7 or Chapter 11, consider the alternatives. Creditors might be willing to settle their claim for a smaller cash payment, or they might be willing to stretch out the loan and reduce the size of the payments. This would allow you to pay off the debt by making smaller payments over a longer period of time. The creditor would eventually receive the full economic benefit of its bargain.

Occasionally, you may "buy time" by consolidating your debts; that is, by taking out a big loan to pay off all the smaller amounts of debts that you owe. The primary danger of this approach is that it is very easy to go out and use your credit cards to borrow even more.

In that case, you end up with an even larger total debt and no more income to meet the monthly payments. Indeed, if you have taken out a second mortgage on your home to obtain the consolidation loan, you might lose your home as well.

When there really is no other way out, you'll need to file for a Chapter 7 personal bankruptcy. Try looking at it in a positive light, however.

There are some advantages to filing for bankruptcy. By far the most important advantage is that debtors may obtain a fresh financial start. Consumers who are eligible for Chapter 7 may be forgiven (discharged from) most unsecured debts.

A secured debt is one which the creditor is entitled to collect by seizing and selling certain assets of the debtor if payments are missed, such as a home mortgage or car loan. With those two major exceptions, most consumer debts are unsecured. You may be able to keep (that is, exempt) many of your assets, although state laws vary widely in defining which assets you may keep.

Collection efforts must stop as soon as you file for bankruptcy under Chapter 7 or Chapter 13. As soon as your petition is filed, there is by law an automatic stay, which prohibits most collection activity.

If a creditor continues to try to collect the debt, the creditor may be cited for contempt of court or ordered to pay damages. The stay applies even to the loan that you may have obtained to buy your car.

If you continue to make payments, it is unlikely that your creditor will do anything. However, if you miss payments your creditor will probably petition to have the stay lifted in order either to repossess the car or to renegotiate the loan.

You cannot be fired from your job solely because you filed for bankruptcy.

Of course, there are disadvantages to filing for bankruptcy. Since your bankruptcy filing will remain on your credit record for up to ten years, it may affect your future finances. A bankruptcy is a troublesome item in your credit record, but often debtors who file already have a troublesome history.

In one respect, bankruptcy may improve your credit records.

Because Chapter 7 provides for a discharge of debts no more than once every eight years, lenders know that a credit applicant who has just emerged from Chapter 7 cannot soon repeat the process.

Research in this area has produced mixed results. A study by the Credit Research Center at Purdue University found that about one-third of consumers who filed for bankruptcy had obtained lines of credit within three years of filing; one-half had obtained them within five years.

However, the new credit itself may reflect the record of bankruptcy. For example, if you might have been eligible for a bank card with a 14 percent rate before bankruptcy, the best card that you can get after bankruptcy might carry a rate of 20 percent—or you might have to rely on a card secured by a deposit that you make with the credit card issuer.

There are a couple of ways you can go about filing for bankruptcy. The most reliable is to secure a bankruptcy attorney and have them do it for you. They are experts in this area and will often take care of everything for you including appearing in court on your behalf.

They do charge a fee for this service, however. That fee can range anywhere from $500 to $2,000 depending on your area. Yes, it is odd that they'll charge that high a fee to file a bankruptcy for someone who doesn't have money in the first place, but many will accept payments.

You can also file the bankruptcy yourself. There are many places on the Internet where you can download the forms you will need. Be advised that they are often lengthy and in-depth, but they are fairly straight-forward when you take the time to fill them out completely.

Once you have the forms all filled out, take them to your local courthouse and pay the filing fee which is usually around $100 to $200. You will receive a notice of a court date at which time you will need to show up and the judge will grant your request for bankruptcy.

The bad part about filing yourself is that you have to contact all your creditors yourself to let them know that the bankruptcy has been filed. You have to be very careful to list each and every one of your debts so they will apply under the discharge order.

If you miss even one, you will have to pay it after the bankruptcy is granted. Filing for bankruptcy might not be your only option. One of the newest trends in achieving financial freedom and a good credit score is to secure the services of a credit counseling or debt consolidation company. But do they work?

Chapter 7
CREDIT COUNSELORS AND DEBT CONSOLIDATORS

These companies have started popping up everywhere. In fact, as I am writing this book, there is a commercial on television for yet another credit counseling company. It seems like they are everywhere. It also seems like they can really help you with your debt problems. But can they?

There are some credit counseling agencies, like Trifecta Financials LLC, and debt consolidators that can actually help get people out of debt. But there are also others who are simply trying to get money without helping you at all.

There is a difference between these two types of companies. Credit counselors will help you get out of debt and stay out of debt. That means that they will help you realize where you went wrong on the financial road and then help you get out of debt. After that, they will put you on a budget and offer services that can help you stay out of debt and live a financially stable life.

Debt consolidation companies are different, though not entirely. They also will help you get out of debt, but they do so by working with your creditors to help combine all of your debts into one large debt with one monthly payment. That usually entails getting some type of loan on your behalf that will pay off your creditors and you will pay the loan company instead.

Because of the services they provide, many people would rather go with a credit counseling service. That's because they need someone to help them stay away from the mindset that got them into debt in the first place. There are many, many credit counseling companies out there.

What do you need to look for in a reputable credit counseling company? Here are a few suggestions:

- They should be associated with the Better Business Bureau. The service's website should have a BBB logo and a link to their record on the Better Business Bureau website. Click through the link to check that there are no unresolved complaints against them.

  Many people only think about the Better Business Bureau after they've been cheated, but by then there's not much you can do. Working with a credit counseling agency that is a member of the Better Business Bureau means that you can go to them to help mediate any dispute you might have with the service provider.

- Reputable credit counseling services will be accredited by an independent nonprofit, just as many schools are. One such accreditation body is the National Institute for financial Counseling Education.

- A good credit counseling agency will charge a small, reasonable monthly fee, usually around $99. Some also charge a fee upfront, though this fee should be reasonable (around $249 tops). It may be possible to get a hardship waiver of these fees if you truly do not have it.

- You will have to fill out an application when you decide to go with a credit counseling agency. The application must clearly say what the fees to be paid are, what the services to be provided are, and in what timeframe all of this will be provided.

Now let's look at how a reputable credit counseling service will work. First, they will negotiate with your creditors to establish a debt management plan (DMP) for you. A DMP may help the debtor repay his or her debt by working out a repayment plan with the creditor.

DMPs, set up by credit counselors, usually offer reduced payments, fees and interest rates to the client. Credit counselors refer to the terms dictated by the creditors to determine payments or interest reductions offered to consumers in a debt management plan.

After joining a DMP, the creditors will close the customer's accounts and restrict the accounts to future charges.

The most common benefit of a DMP as advertised by most agencies is the consolidation of multiple monthly payments into just one monthly payment which is usually less than the sum of the individual payment previously paid by the customer.

This is because the credit card banks will usually accept a lower monthly payment from a customer in a DMP than if the customer were paying the account on their own. Some DMPs advertise that payments can be cut by 50 % although a reduction of 10 to 20 percent is more common.

The second feature of a DMP is a reduction in interest rates charged by creditors. A customer with a defaulted credit card account will often be paying an interest rate approaching 30 percent. Upon joining a DMP, credit card banks sometimes lower the annual percentage rates charged to 5 to 10 percent and a few will eliminate the interest altogether.

This reduction in interest allows the counseling agencies to advertise that their customers will be debt free in periods of three to six years rather than the twenty plus years that it would take to pay off a large amount of debt at high interest rates. That's a very attractive advantage – especially for people who are in debt quite a bit.

A third benefit offered by credit counseling agencies is the process of bringing delinquent accounts current. This is often called "re-aging" or "curing" an account. This usually occurs after making a series of on-time payments through the DMP as a show of good faith and commitment to completion of the program. For example, a client with an account that has a monthly payment of $50 but that monthly payment has not been paid in two months might be considered by the creditor to be 60 days past due. After joining the DMP and making three consecutive on-time monthly payments, the creditor could "re-age" the account to reflect a current status.

After that, the monthly payment due on the statements would be the monthly payment negotiated by the DMP and the account would be reported as current to the credit bureaus. Now this process does not eliminate the prior delinquencies from the credit reports. What is does is merely give a fresh start and opportunity for the client to begin building a positive credit history. Like all negative credit information, only the passage of time will lessen the impact of the negative marks when credit scores are calculated.

So how do credit counseling companies make money? They do charge a fee to you for their services, and it is important for you to get all of that information in writing before you sign on the dotted line. However, this fee is not usually enough to make them a huge profit.

The credit counseling companies make most of their compensation from the creditors to whom the debt payments are distributed. This funding relationship has led many to believe that credit counseling agencies are merely a collections wing of the creditors.

This fee income, known as "fair Share," consists of contributions from the creditors that originally earned the agency 15% of the amount recovered. However, in recent years, fair Share contributions have dwindled steadily, with contributions of 4-10% being the most common.

There is a lot of criticism, in fact, when it comes to credit counseling agencies and their effectiveness as well as legality. The federal Trade Commission has filed lawsuits against several credit counseling agencies, and they continue to urge caution to consumers when it comes to choosing a credit counseling agency.

The FTC has received over 8,000 complaints from consumers about shady credit counselors. Many of those complaints concern high or hidden fees along with the inability to opt out of so-called "voluntary" contributions. The Better Business Bureau also reports high complaint levels about credit counseling.

Not surprisingly, the IRS has also weighed in on the subject of credit counseling and has denied non-profit, tax-exempt status to around thirty of the nation's 1,000 credit counseling agencies. Those thirty agencies account for more than half of the industry's revenue. Audits of non-profit credit counseling agencies by the IRS are ongoing.

The lobby against credit counselors arises from the belief by the collection industry that the not-for-profit status of the credit counselors gives them an unfair financial and market advantage over them. The IRS apparently agrees.

The tax-exempt revocations seem to be centered on whether or not a tax-exempt credit counselor actually performed their mandated mission by assisting the community at large as opposed to offering their whole attention to their own DMP customers in a "collection practice". However, that has yet to be proven.

Congress has also investigated the credit counseling industry and has issued a report that says while some agencies are ethical, others charge excessive fees and provide poor service to consumers.

The report also states that NFCC member guidelines, if applied to the entire industry, would go a long way toward eliminating the abuses they have uncovered in other parts of the industry.

When it comes to debt consolidation companies, you are talking about an entirely different concept. What a debt consolidation company does is negotiate with creditors to get a lower pay-off amount for your debts and then obtain a loan on your behalf to pay off those creditors allowing you to make just one payment instead of multiple ones.

The two types of companies are similar in nature, but with debt consolidation, the only thing they do is negotiate with credit lenders and then get you one payment instead of many. They do charge a fee for their services as well just as the credit counseling companies do.

The thing about debt consolidation companies is that they do what you can do yourself with just a little bit of work. You can call your creditors and negotiate a pay-off balance for your accounts and then obtain your own loan as a debt consolidation loan. Even if you have less than perfect credit, most banks and lending institutions will have debt consolidation loans available to almost everyone.

Really, the bottom line when considering either a debt consolidation company or a credit counselor is to weight the advantages and disadvantages first. Then check out the company you are considering, make sure they are reputable.

These types of companies can really and truly help people who are seriously in debt. But proceed with caution and choose wisely lest you get yourself involved in yet another problem besides your debt!

Now that we've addressed no credit, bad credit, and people who can help with credit problems, let's focus on your credit report and your credit score. Often, there are mistakes that are on your credit report, and correcting them is essential.

Chapter 8
MISTAKES CAN BE MADE

As we've said before, your credit report is very important to you as well as your credit score. People are human and the information contained in your credit report is entered in by human hands. Sometimes those hands make mistakes.

Maybe you paid off a past due bill and it's still showing on your credit report as delinquent. There are all sorts of things that can be reflected incorrectly on your credit report, so it's important that you take steps to make corrections as soon as you can.

The first thing you need to do is check over your report and dispute any old negative reports you can find. Say that fight with your phone company over an unfair bill a few years ago resulted in a collections account. You can continue protesting that the charge was unjust, or you can try disputing the account with the credit bureaus as "not mine."

The older and smaller a collection account, the more likely the collection agency won't bother to verify it when the credit bureau investigates your dispute. Some consumers also have had luck disputing old items with a lender that has merged with another company, which can leave lender records a real mess.

If there are significant errors on your credit report, you need to be sure and get them removed right away. However, there are also some mistakes that you can ignore, and it won't impact you negatively.

Your credit score is calculated based on the information in your credit report, so certain errors there can really cost you. But not everything that's reported in your file matters to your score.

Here's the stuff that's usually worth the effort of correcting with the bureaus:

- Late payments, charge-offs, collections or other negative items that aren't yours.
- Credit limits reported as lower than they actually are.
- Accounts listed as "settled," "paid derogatory," "paid charge-off" or anything other than "current" or "paid as agreed" if you paid on time and in full.

- Accounts that are still listed as unpaid that was included in a bankruptcy.
- Negative items older than seven years (10 in the case of bankruptcy) that should have automatically fallen off your report.

You actually have to be a bit careful with this last one, because sometimes scores actually go down when bad items fall off your report. It's a quirk in the FICO credit-scoring software, and the potential effect of eliminating old negative items is difficult to predict in advance.

Some of the stuff that you typically shouldn't worry about includes:

- Various misspellings of your name.
- Outdated or incorrect address information.
- An old employer listed as current.
- Most inquiries.

If the misspelled name or incorrect address is because of identity theft or because your file has been mixed with someone else's, that should be obvious when you look at your accounts. You'll see delinquencies or accounts that aren't yours and should report that immediately.

However, if it's just a goof by the credit bureau or one of the companies reporting to it, it's usually not much to sweat about. Two more items you don't need to correct:

- Accounts you closed listed as being open.
- Accounts you closed that don't say "closed by consumer."

Closing accounts can't help your score; and may hurt it. If your goal is boosting your score, leave these alone. Once an account has been closed, though, it doesn't matter to the scoring formulas that did it -- you or the lender. If you messed up the account, it will be obvious from the late payments and other derogatory information included in the file.

So, say you've found some significant errors on your credit report and you need to correct them. There are certain steps you need to take in order to make sure that the error is corrected and ultimately removed from your report.

1. Make a copy of your credit report and circle every item you believe is incorrect.

2. Write a letter to the reporting agency (the address will be printed on the report). Explain each dispute and request an investigation to resolve the issues. If you have supporting paperwork, send it along, coding pages to match dispute paragraphs. Do not send your originals.

3. Send all materials by certified mail, return receipt requested, so that you can prove the packet was received.

4. Send a similar letter of dispute to the creditor whose reporting statements you disagree with. Refer to a billing statement to find the correct address for disputes, because it's usually different from the payment address.

If your dispute involves personal information, such as your current address, enclose a copy of your driver's license or a utility bill in your name to verify your residence. The reporting agency will initiate an investigation, contacting your creditors to verify the accuracy of the information. If the creditor cannot verify that the entry is correct, it must be removed. When the investigation is complete, the agency must send you a free copy of your report if changes were made.

If the investigation uncovers an error, you have the right to ask that a corrected version of your credit report be sent to everyone who received the report during the past six months. It's a good idea to contact your creditor first, then allow a bit of lead time before you submit the dispute to the reporting agency. By the time the dispute is verified, the creditor will hopefully have corrected the error.

You can also make changes online directly with the credit reporting agency. When you are on their website, they will usually have links that allow you to click a button to dispute incorrect information. You can initiate an investigation from many online credit reports by following the links provided and checking the disputed items as directed. There sometimes isn't a place for remarks--you'll simply check a multiple-choice reason for each dispute.

If the credit reporting agency says the original information is accurate, it must provide you with a written notice that includes the name, address, and phone number of the person who made the report. If you still disagree, initiate a second investigation.

Unfortunately, in the real world the reporting agencies often try to sidestep that requirement, giving you standard, computer-generated information rather than the facts you need to find the person or department who made the negative report. Keep plugging away until you have the answer you're looking for.

If your attempts to correct an entry are unsuccessful, you can ask the reporting agency to insert a 100-character explanation next to it that explains your side of the story. Under the Fair Credit Reporting Act, the credit bureau is required to solve the problem in a reasonable amount of time, generally 30 days. If you feel that a credit bureau has not responded promptly and fairly to your situation, contact the attorney general of your state or The Federal Trade Commission in Washington at (202) FTC-HELP.

If you are disputing something on your credit report, you might want to try the following sample letter in your attempts:

YOUR NAME
YOUR ADDRESS
YOUR CITY, STATE, ZIP CODE

COMPLAINT DEPARTMENT
NAME Of COMPANY
ADDRESS
CITY, STATE, ZIP CODE

DATE

Dear Sir or Madam:

I am writing to dispute the following information in my file. The items dispute also are encircled on the attached copy of the report I received.

This item (identify item(s) disputed by name of source, such as creditors or tax court, and identify type of item, such as credit account, judgment, etc.) is (inaccurate or incomplete) because (describe what is inaccurate or incomplete and why). I am requesting that the item be deleted (or request another specific change) to correct the information.

Another great reason for keeping tabs on your credit report as much as possible is the possibility of identity theft. It happens all the time and often the only way you will know it has happened to you is to check your credit report.

Chapter 9
IDENTITY THEFT AND YOUR CREDIT

Criminals know the way to steal your identity, and the worst part is that it's not all that difficult. You know all those credit card applications you get in the mail? If you don't shred them, they can use that to steal your identity.

It's not above them to sift through garbage just to obtain a social security number or a driver's license number. Once they have these vital bits of information, it's easy for them to steal your identity. What they will do is scary. They will apply for credit cards in your name and max them out within days. They will obtain loans in your name and never make a payment. Then the loan company comes after you for the money. It's something that affects millions and millions of people each year and it can be a real mess when it comes to your credit report.

As many as 85 percent of all identity theft victims find out about the crime only when they are denied credit or employment, contacted by the police, or have to deal with collection agencies, credit cards, and bills. A study on the aftermath of an identity theft by the nonprofit Identity Theft Resource Center found that victims spend 600 hours recovering from the crime because they must contact and work with credit cards, banks, credit bureaus, and law enforcement. The time can add up to as much as $16,000 in lost wages or income.

The number of reported cases of identity theft is increasing steadily. There is no one reason for this, but rather this is due to several ways in which our lives have changed in recent years, all of which make it easier for people to obtain our personal information. In the United States, Social Security numbers are used more commonly as a means of identification. The Internet has made the transmission of personal information easy and, at times, less secure. Online retailers store our credit card information and contact information in databases we assume to be secured.

Marketing databases not only contain personal information, but they aggregate information on our spending habits as well as contact information. But potentially nefarious employees of these companies could have access to that information.

They can then sell it online in chat rooms where criminals meet to swap information. Even in the days of e-mail and instant messaging, the postal mail can also play a surprising role in identity theft. Checks can be stolen from the outgoing mail. Credit card companies bombard their customers and potential customers with pre-approved offers that need very little personal information to complete.

Credit card issuers also send what they call "courtesy checks" to customers who can use them to make charges on a card. Many experts consider them an invitation to identity theft. One of the increasingly common ways that criminals try to obtain personal information is by using what is called a "phishing attack." If you have e-mail, the chances are good someone has tried to get you to bite.

Phishing combines a criminal attempt at obtaining personal information with another plague of the Internet age — spam. Potential victims receive an e-mail from what appears to be a bank, an online payment company like PayPal, or a retailer like eBay or Amazon.com. The message is usually sent using html e-mail and, when opened, uses company logos and symbols to make it appear to be legitimate.

The e-mail asks the receiver for their usernames, passwords, account numbers, or some other type of personal information by saying they are updating records, or something related to their account requires their attention. The e-mail usually links to a site that also appears to be legitimate using logos and other symbols of a real company, where visitors are asked to supply the information.

The first step to avoid becoming the victim of a phishing attack is to know what companies do business with you by e-mail and familiarizing yourself with the types information they request and how they request it. What you will likely learn quickly is that, while online retailers you frequent and financial services firms you use online often send you e-mail to make you aware of new products or services, or even to alert you when your online bill is ready to be viewed, they rarely if ever ask for any information from you.

Banks and financial services firms will never ask you for any personal information via e-mail, because e-mail can be notoriously insecure. Any e-mail asking you for personal or account information, such as passwords, Social Security numbers, PINs, credit or check card numbers, or other confidential information should be deemed suspicious.

Often the sender of a phishing e-mail may appear to be legitimate, but e-mail addresses are easily spoofed. Just look at the amount of spam you probably get that appears to be from friends, co-workers, or even yourself.

If a phishing e-mail directs you to a link using an html e-mail, the text of the link may appear to be legitimate, but following that link often brings you to a Web site where the URL (in your web browser's location bar) is often an IP address (basically numbers separated by periods, like 128.0.0) or a site other than the institution you think sent you the e-mail.

Often a sense of urgency is conveyed in the e-mail, such as an alert saying your account will be closed if you don't provide information. Take a moment and don't fall for this. A close look at the body of the e-mail itself may reveal typos, misspellings, or horrendously poor grammar. One reason for this is that many phishing attacks are launched from overseas, and many are believed to be related to international organized crime.

Despite all the attention phishing has received of late, there remains precious little enforcement of the widespread problem and there are simply too many attacks to handle. It is an easy buck for online criminals. We already covered many of the ways you can detect a phishing attack, but there are several simple steps you can take to keep your private information safe that bear discussion. Experts say that educating consumers not to follow links in e-mails is a good way to help them avoid phishing attacks. Rather than following a link in an e-mail, open a browser and go to the site of the retailer or bank in question.

When submitting personal information like credit card numbers, you can ensure you are using a secure connection by looking for "https://" in front of the site's location on your browser rather than "http://."

Speaking of your browser, make sure it is up to date with the latest security patches. If you use Microsoft's Internet Explorer, visit WindowsUpdate.com to see if you need any updates. Here are some simple software tools you can use to help guard against online identity theft:

- CoreStreet makes a free product called SpoofStick. It's a browser extension for both the Internet Explorer and Firefox Web browsers that helps users avoid spoofed web sites. If you do follow a link in a suspicious e-mail, SpoofStick can tell you if the Web site you visit really is the Web site you think you are visiting.

- The Earthlink toolbar, which is also free to Internet users, has a feature called ScamBlocker. Earthlink keeps a database of known phishers, and if you visit a page known to be operated by a phisher it will alert you right in your browser.

Unfortunately, correcting your credit report when you have become a victim of identity theft is no easy proposition. But with some patience and a lot of work, you can recover from identity theft and restore your credit report.

Identity theft can result in damage to your credit rating - damage that could take years to fix. Generally, victims of credit and banking fraud are liable for no more than the first $50 of the loss. In many cases, the victim will not be required to pay any part of the loss.

To reduce your risk of identity theft, protect personal information and do not carry your Social Security card with you. Shred items that contain your personal information and account numbers. Keep your mail safe and store your personal information in a safe place. Order your credit report at least once a year to make sure no one is using your identity to open accounts.

If you think your identity has been stolen, take the following steps:

- Contact the three major credit bureaus - Contact the fraud departments of all of the three major credit departments to place a fraud alert on your credit file. The initial fraud alert is for 90 days. You can ask for an extended fraud alert if you file a police report.
- Close accounts - Close the accounts that you know or believe have been tampered with or opened fraudulently.
- File a police report - Get a copy of the report to submit to your creditors and others who require proof of the crime.
- File your complaint with the Federal Trade Commission (FTC) - The FTC maintains a database of identity theft cases, which is used by law enforcement agencies for investigations. Filing a complaint also helps us learn more about identity theft and the problems it causes victims.
- Armed with your police report, FTC affidavit, and sample letters - you must contact your creditors to alert them to the situation. In addition to obvious creditors like your credit card issuers, don't forget utility companies, wireless phone provider, and your ISP.

When you are trying to correct your credit report due to identity theft, you will have to provide information that proves you are you. That means digging out your birth certificate and making a lot of copies of your driver's license and social security card. You'll also have to try and prove that you didn't make the purchases that the thief or thieves did.

When you have become a victim of identity theft through phishing, this becomes a real problem as these purchases can be made anywhere with a few strokes of the keyboard, so proving that the purchases were made by someone other than you can be a real headache. Just try to be patient and point out to the company or companies who say you owe them money that you have filed a police report as well as a report with the FTC and that you have been a victim in other places as well.

Chapter 10
RAISING YOUR CREDIT SCORE

Let's say you want to buy a house, but your credit score is somewhere around 675 instead of 720, you will not get the best rate on that home loan. If you want to raise your credit score quickly, there are some steps you can take that can guarantee a great home loan or any other credit line for that matter. The mantra for getting a great score is pay your bills on time, keep account balances low, and take out new credit only when you need it. People who do that faithfully have very high scores. It usually means you're being conservative and cautious about credit. It's not a toy and it shouldn't be a hobby.

That's good advice, to be sure, but these actions take a long time. What if you're house hunting and you just need a few extra points to bump you over the line to the great rates? As we've said before, the first place to start is with your credit report. Check it over and find out what your credit score is right now.

You will want to concentrate mostly on correcting any errors by taking the steps we've outlined above. Look for errors such as accounts that aren't yours, late payments that were actually paid on time, debts you paid off that are shown as outstanding, or old debts that shouldn't be reported any longer.

Negatives are supposed to be deleted after seven years, with the exception of bankruptcies, which can stay for as long as 10 years. After repairing errors, the fastest route to a better score is paying down balances on credit cards. There's really no silver bullet, but over a 60-day time period, it is possible to increase your score 20 points by paying down your credit lines.

Had a few late payments in your past? If you find yourself in some financial difficulties, you can protect your score by making sure your payments don't go 60 days past due. Some lenders don't report 30 days past due, but they all report 60 days past due. Even if you've paid your bills late in the past, you can improve your credit score by paying every bill on time from now on. If you need further assistance go to www.trifectafinancials.com and get s FREE credit analysis.

One thing you shouldn't do if you're just trying to boost your score is close unused accounts. If someone tells you to close unused accounts to improve your score, they're pulling your leg. It won't help you and it can actually hurt you.

Closing unused accounts without paying down your debt changes your utilization ratio, which is the amount of your total debt divided by your total available credit. You appear closer to maxing out your accounts. That's why your score can drop. It doesn't mean people shouldn't close them, but don't close them to improve your score.

If you do cut up cards, though, leave the oldest one open. The length of your credit history is another factor in your score. If you close the account of the credit card you got when you were a freshman in college and leave open the ones you just got within the last couple years, it makes you look like a much newer borrower.

Another strategy for bringing up your score is to transfer balances from a card that's close to being maxed out to other cards to even out your usage. You can also just spread out your charges between a few cards. Try to get the usage on all of them at 20 to 30 percent instead of a bunch at zero and one at 80 percent. You're not spending less; you're just shifting it around to different cards.

Transferring the balance to a card with a lower utilization could help, but it's much better to actually pay down the debt if you have the cash kicking around.

If you're really into finessing the system, check your credit report to see what day of the month your creditors send updates on payments to the credit bureaus. They're rarely on the same cycle as your payment due date. That's why you can pay off your card every month and your credit report will show you carrying a balance. Try to make your payments several days before the reporting date.

All of these strategies generally take at least 30 days because lenders don't report payments more than once a month.

If you're in the throes of qualifying for a mortgage and need a score boost in a hurry, you can speed the process along with rapid rescoring. If you've got legitimate negative information on your credit report, such as late payments or accounts in collections, you're out of luck. But the process of rapid rescoring can help increase your score within a few days by correcting errors or paying off account balances.

You can't do this one yourself; you'll need a lender who is a customer of a rapid rescoring service such as Trifecta Financials LLC. Generally, the service will run roughly $50 for every account on your credit report that needs to be addressed, but it could save you thousands on your loan. If a consumer can find a lender who is a customer of a rapid rescoring service, new information can be posted within 72 hours.

There's a lot of information that we've presented to you in previous section, so let's do a little recap on the more important points.

Chapter 11
OVERALL REVIEW

The very first thing that you must do in order to raise your credit score is to order your free annual credit report and find out what your credit score is. Once you have obtained copies of your credit reports from all three credit reporting agencies: Experian, Equifax, and TransUnion, you must take the time to go over those reports to check for errors and inconsistencies. It is imperative that you correct any mistakes or inconsistencies as soon as possible. This is the most pro-active step you can take for yourself to increase your credit score as mistakes can and do happen.

Look for accounts that were previously delinquent, but which have since been paid off. Find any accounts that were closed or any accounts that aren't yours. Then take steps to correct those errors by contacting the credit bureaus and beginning the process in writing to have these errors removed from the report. This alone can raise your credit score.

Checking your credit report often can also indicate if you have become a victim of identity theft which is something that is happening over and over again with frightening frequency. It affects millions of people and can wreak havoc with your credit rating. Correcting the problem of identity theft is a process that will take quite some time, but it can be done with patience and excellent documentation. You should definitely be contacting the FTC and filing a police report in this situation so that your credibility cannot be called into question.

In the above section, we discussed extensively the option of filing for bankruptcy. This should be done only as a last resort and if you are in dire financial straits that cannot be solved if you just don't have the means to pay off your debts.

Filing for bankruptcy doesn't have the stigma attached to it that it once did and is nothing to be ashamed of. While it's true that the bankruptcy will remain on your credit report for up to ten years, lenders know that you will not be able to file for bankruptcy again within that time frame, so you may actually be able to obtain credit anyway after a bankruptcy.

Before you resort to a bankruptcy filing, you can first try getting the advice of a credit counselor to help get you back on track when it comes to your money problems. Trifecta Financials LLC offer FREE assistance at www.trifectafinancials.com.

Credit counseling companies not only work with your creditors to secure lower repayment rates, but they provide financial planning advice for you to use in the future, so you are not put in the same situation you were in before. If you do have steady income, you may want to look into a debt consolidation loan. That way you can pay off your creditors and make one monthly payment to one company instead of several monthly payments to several companies.

There are also companies who can help with debt consolidation loans although you can certainly do it on your own. They can, however, secure loans for you with a lower interest rate and shop around to different companies to find you the best debt consolidation loan and help you get out of debt.

If you have bad credit, expect to take about a year or two to get it up to a better credit rating; or Trifecta Financials LLC can increase it in 90 days. If you choose to do it on your own here are a few steps to follow:

- Pay your bills on time- This alone will show good faith to your creditors and have a positive effect on your credit rating
- Don't use credit at all if possible- That means cutting up your credit cards and paying cash for the things you need.
- You may want to keep one credit card that you can use for emergencies – but remember that it is for emergencies only. Keep the oldest card you have as that shows you are not newly applying for credit.
- A good idea for not using that one credit card is to freeze it in a block of ice. It won't damage the card and it will require thawing before you can use it. That way, you will have to wait before making a purchase thus eliminating the lure of an impulse purchase.
- Don't apply for new lines of credit at all! The only time you should ever be applying for credit when you are financial straits is if you need to make a big purchase such as a vehicle or home.
- Monitor your credit report faithfully and immediately correct any mistakes that you find.

- If you find that you cannot make a payment on time, call your creditor and explain the circumstances. If you have been a good customer, they may be willing to accept a late payment and waive the late fees. Try not to do this too often as it can reflect poorly on your payment history.
- If you have little to no credit, you can establish credit by obtaining a department store or gas credit card. Then you make a few purchases and pay the balance off immediately.
- Be very careful when making purchases online. Make sure that when you are entering in your credit card number it is done on a web site that starts with https://. The "s" at the end of the http designation shows that it is a secure sight that will keep your information private.
- Beware of "phishing" e-mails that direct you to a separate site where you are asked to provide personal information. This is how many identity thieves obtain your bank account or credit card numbers and they can run up horrendous bills in a few moments of time.
- If you want to obtain a large loan as for a vehicle, you may want to try and get a co- signer who has good credit. Their good name and credit history can help you get the loan and build your credit at the same time.
- Again, we want to iterate the most important thing about maintaining good credit and raising your credit score: MAKE YOUR PAYMENTS ON TIME! And use credit sparingly.

There are a lot of great tools available online to help you with credit and making credit decisions. Go to www.myfico.com and check out some of their calculators. Since FICO is the company who assigns you that magic little number that is your credit score, they are a great source of help for the consumer. At this site, you can find out:

- Which loan is better?
- How much your mortgage payments will be
- How much money you can afford to borrow?
- Whether or not you are better off refinancing a loan
- How much refinancing costs will be?
- Whether or not you should consolidate your credit cards
- How long it will take to pay off a credit card balance
- How rate changes will affect your loan balance and much, much more!

You can also find many other websites that can help guide you through not only the credit process but how to get and maintain a solid credit score and rating. Last, but not least, don't forget the three major credit card reporting agencies. These are the places you should start to obtain your credit report and get on your way toward better credit.

- Experian: www.experian.com
- TransUnion: www.transunion.com
- Equifax: www.equifax.com

Plus, you can also go to the following websites to obtain your annual free credit report that is available once a year to all consumers:

- www.annualcreditreport.com
- www.freecreditreport.com

CONCLUSION

Like we said at the beginning of this book, we are a country in debt. Our "money" is "debt notes" as stated on them. While it might not be the best way to think about it, when the price of things like vehicles and homes is well beyond what we would be able to pay cash for, we have to face the reality that it is true!

In all actuality, the concept of credit has actually been around for a very long time, just the people in power never allowed us to be taught about it in school. I read this description in a book and I believe it fits what I am trying to say.

Anyone who is a fan of "little House on the Prairie" knows that when the Ingalls would go to the general store, they would always put their items "on account" which would be paid later – usually when the crops were in or Paw got paid from his various jobs.

Back then, credit reports and credit scores weren't necessary. It was an unwritten rule that the accounts would eventually be paid. A man's word was his name and their name meant everything back then. Collection agencies weren't necessary, and accounts always got paid even if took some time. The shop owners didn't worry and were willing to wait. It was the law of the settlers albeit and unwritten one!

As time passed, accounts weren't being paid and businesses were asked to take hits from people who reneged on their agreements. This brings us to where we are today: a nation in debt. Even the federal Government is in debt. It only goes to follow that citizens would be in debt too.

That said, we know we need credit to obtain the things we need – and often those that we don't. Credit card companies are preying on people at a younger and younger age. That puts young people alarmingly in debt before they even get to the legal drinking age.

That's why it's so important to know about credit and when it should be used as well as when it shouldn't be used. Practice smart credit procedures and don't overextend yourself. You can easily find yourself in trouble before you even know it.
Then the time comes to change your spending habits, make smart credit decisions and take steps to raise your credit score.

No matter what situation you might find yourself in regarding your credit, you can not only get out of debt, but you can restore your credit and enjoy a high credit score. It takes time and a little bit of effort, but it certainly can be done. You just need to be diligent about your spending habits and then monitor your credit reports, so you know where you stand at any particular time.

Credit is an important part of our society, so cherish your credit history and your credit score. Make it just as important to you as your good name and keep it clean and pristine. It can mean so much to your future and your future is just as important as the present.

If you need assistance, Trifecta Financials LLC offers FREE assistance to all. They also offer dispute letters in their "Resource" area at: www.trifectafinancials.com

LEGAL NOTICE